# LATE EGYPTIAN AND COPTIC ART

# LATE EGYPTIAN AND

# COPTIC ART

AN INTRODUCTION TO THE COLLECTIONS

IN THE BROOKLYN MUSEUM

1943

BROOKLYN MUSEUM

BROOKLYN INSTITUTE OF ARTS AND SCIENCES

# FOREWORD

THE Coptic collection covered by this guide has recently been placed on exhibition in the former Classical Court, adjoining the Wilbour Hall, on the third floor of the Museum. The beginnings of the collection date back to the earliest days of the Museum. In 1898 the Egyptian Department was founded with the acquisition of a mummy and a fragment of a Coptic wool tunic, the latter the gift of the enthusiastic Amelia B. Edwards, the pioneer woman egyptologist, well known throughout the United States for her books and lectures. Within a few months the Egypt Exploration Society gave some late Egypto-Roman bronzes from the Faiyûm, the first of a long series of gifts from that Society's excavations. In 1905, Sir Flinders Petrie selected a few Coptic pieces in Egypt for the Brooklyn collection and from time to time the Trustees purchased others.

But until 1915 the Brooklyn Coptic collection was little more than a small group of unrelated objects. In that year, Colonel Robert B. Woodward gave a large collection of Coptic textiles from the excavations of the Egypt Exploration Society at Antinoë; and from that time the collections grew rapidly. In 1916 the Museum received, as a gift of the children of Charles Edwin Wilbour, the collection formed by him in Egypt from 1882 to 1896. While the bulk of the Wilbour collection represented earlier periods, Mr. Wilbour was deeply interested in the then ignored Coptic period and had acquired numerous Coptic items, some of them of outstanding quality. The Long Island Historical Society presented, in 1926, a collection of Coptic objects, including some particularly fine textiles. More recently Pratt Institute has greatly enriched the textile collection by gifts and permanent loans from the fine group of Coptic pieces assembled many years ago by Mr. Frederic B. Pratt. The Pratt collection includes several unique designs.

The Trustees have, in recent years, purchased outstanding Coptic works of art, usually from the income of the Charles Edwin Wilbour Fund, with the purpose of making the Egyptian collections of the Museum representative of the entire range of ancient Egyptian culture. Today the collection is still small and does not completely cover the field, for Coptic objects are rare; but it contains some of the finest Coptic sculptures and bronzes to be found outside of Egypt, and, if used in connection with the resources of the Wilbour Library, which houses most of the all-too-limited published material on Coptic civilization, it will give the visitor a good survey of Coptic art.

## NOTE TO VISITORS

Visitors who would like to refer to books or illustrations bearing on the collections covered by this guide will find material on all phases of Egyptian civilization in the Charles Edwin Wilbour Memorial Library adjacent to the Egyptian Galleries on the third floor of the Museum. The librarian will be glad to recommend books or to compile bibliographies on special subjects.

# INTRODUCTION

THE history of late Egyptian and Coptic art covers the long period from about 300 B. C. to the middle of the seventh century after Christ. For our purpose the period may be divided into two groups, the first extending from 300 B. C. to the beginning of the fourth century after Christ. It is usually called the Graeco-Roman period. The other, and artistically much the more important period, extends from the early fourth century to the time of the Arab conquest of Egypt in the middle of the seventh century. This is the Coptic period, the time when Egypt was a Christian nation.

The Graeco-Roman age commenced with the conquest of Egypt by Alexander the Great, who was soon succeeded by one of his Greek generals, Ptolemy, the founder of the Ptolemaic Dynasty (323-30 B. C.). The days of Egypt's greatness as an independent nation were over, and she was in her dotage. The Greek kings tolerated the ancient religion and made an outward show of observing native customs, but their education and instincts were Greek, and inevitably a veneer of Greek culture was spread over the entire land.

The capital of Egypt was the fabulous Alexandria, for centuries the greatest city of the world, larger by far than republican Rome. Alexandria was a Greek city set in Egypt. Her buildings and sculptures in the Greek style were famous throughout the western world, and she established Greek art and civilization as the successors of the ancient Egyptian culture. The ancient arts and crafts did not disappear at once, but they survived in an utterly lifeless manner, only rarely producing something of character. With these survivals of the ancient culture we are not here concerned; for they are exhibited in the Egyptian galleries.

Little has been spared to us of the glory of early Alexandrian art, and the period is poorly represented in American collections. One fine example in Brooklyn, illustrated on Pls. 5 and 6, is typical of the school. It is a head of the chief Greek god, Zeus, in the rather exuberant style of late Greek art. The stone, style and workmanship are Greek, but the horns of a ram, the animal sacred to the chief Egyptian god Amon, have been added. Such applied Egyptian detail is characteristic of the Alexandrian school. The bronzes in Pls. 23 and 24 are good examples of later Alexandrian art.

Alexandrian art is important in the history of Egyptian art, not for its productions, of which too few examples have survived for us to possess a representative selection, but for the Greek influence it imposed on Egypt. This Greek tradition, the legacy of Alexandria, influenced Egyptian art until the sixth century after Christ, a period of almost one thousand years.

The romantic episode of Antony and Cleopatra marked the downfall of the Ptolemaic Dynasty and ushered in the rule of Rome. This political change did not destroy the Greek basis of later Egyptian culture. What influence Roman art had in Alexandria, if any, we do not know; but throughout the rest of Egypt it made a noticeable impression, and both the Alexandrian and Roman styles were popular during the first centuries of Roman rule. These were not the only influences at work in Egypt during this cosmopolitan period, for the Nile valley was the melting pot of the Near East, with many foreign cults and arts gaining followers there. While minor influences are frequently found in pieces made in the ancient Egyptian style, they made no lasting impression on Egyptian art. With rare exceptions, the Roman period in Egypt produced no great art and is marked by the rapid decline both in craftsmanship and in the quantity of objects produced.

The Faiyûm- or mummy-portraits are probably the most beautiful objects that have come down to us from the Roman period in Egypt. Painted from life, usually in a wax technique, they are the earliest surviving painted panel portraits, and give us a vivid impression of the appearance of the Greek settlers in Egypt. For the most part the portraits represent well-to-do Greeks, whose features betray the Oriental influences already so apparent in their culture. These portraits were apparently usually painted during the lifetime of the subject, and hung on the wall of his house; after his death, they were cut down to fit on the body, mummified and bandaged in the Egyptian style. This custom was based on the ancient Egyptian practice of placing an idealized portrait-mask over the face of the mummy. The use of painted portraits on mummies seems to have been limited to small groups of Greeks, mainly in the Faiyûm, a fertile region not far south of Cairo, thickly populated by foreigners. The portraits date principally over the first three centuries after Christ, although examples from the fourth century are known.

For those who could not afford the luxury of a portrait, an inexpensive substitute was the painted plaster mask, examples of which are exhibited in the gallery. Most of these masks show some attempt at portraiture and almost all of them were vividly, if not gaudily, painted. They were, of course, purely funerary pieces, made to be placed on the cover of the coffin. In their stark realism they are closer to Roman than to Greek art and the elaborate coiffures of some of the later specimens recall Roman portrait-busts. They were in use for about the same period as the painted portraits.

In ancient Egypt, sculpture had been the most important and characteristic art of the country, but during the Roman period sculpture in the round becomes very rare, finally petering out entirely. A few temple statues were produced, along with sculptures of the ruling emperor, but they are rare and cease entirely after the late third century. However, small sculptures or statuettes of gods increase enormously during the early centuries of the Roman period. We no longer find the slender and elegant forms of the great Egyptian deities nor the familiar gods of Greek Alexandria. Instead we find vast masses of weird and unfamiliar beings in terra-cotta and soft stones: fantastic combinations of animals, reptiles and humans; familiar Egyptian gods such as Horus, Isis and Bes, but often so changed in appearance that at first we do not recognize them. Only rarely do these statuettes have any art interest. They are of importance, however, in showing the many influences at work in Egypt and the background against which Christianity was to triumph.

The Egyptians of the Roman period continued the ancient custom of erecting stelae, or tombstones, to their dead. In ancient Egypt these tombstones had the very practical purpose of supplying the deceased with food and the necessities of daily life for use in the next world, by virtue of magical texts incised on them. Now, their chief purpose seems to be commemorative, following the Greek custom, and, in place of magical texts, we find only names and genealogies and sometimes a conventional phrase of farewell. Many foreign influences are apparent on these tombstones, and the meanings of some compositions are as yet unknown to us. Their use continued throughout the Coptic period.

Bronze-casting and goldwork were two crafts which maintained high standards in this period, and both rare and typical specimens of these crafts are exhibited in the gallery. Of particular interest, and comparative rarity, are the bronze altars, probably of Egyptian manufacture, showing Roman and Syrian influence. Similar specimens have been found throughout the Near East. Other bronzes, the fine patera for example, were certainly imported.

From this brief survey of the Graeco-Roman period in Egypt one important point is clear: culturally, or artistically, the country was not unified. Foreign rule had completely undermined the native culture without entirely replacing it. The tradition of Alexandrian art continued to influence some of the many local schools, probably those in Lower Egypt, but Roman and Near Eastern influences were almost equally powerful. Many foreigners had settled in Egypt during the Ptolemaic and Roman periods, bringing with them their gods and arts, adding to the confusion of late Egyptian civilization. The numerous conflicting religions required cult objects, frequently so combined with earlier forms that at present it is usually impossible to unravel the various influences.

Our knowledge of Egypt in the later Roman period is extremely vague. It was an age of economic decline. Roman dominion had drained Egypt's resources and her comparative poverty is reflected in the poor and reduced art output. But it was during this dark period that the basis was formed for Egypt's next great age, the Coptic period. Although we know but little of its beginnings, the impulse for this new art seems to have come from within the country. Like most cultures, it bears the imprint of foreign influences and, in particular, it shares in the shift of the entire Mediterranean world of the period towards a conventionalized art.

The gradual conversion of Egypt to Christianity gave that religion the dominant cultural position in the country, and during its ascendency a new and unified art began to appear. This is the art of the Copts, the name given to the Egyptians who embraced Christianity. While a few Coptic objects, almost exclusively textiles, can be assigned to the third century, it is doubtful if the use of "Coptic" is justified before the fourth century, and even from that period there is little that is characteristic of the new style. The golden age of Coptic art was the fifth and sixth centuries.

Logically, "Coptic" should be applied only to the productions of Egyptian Christians. For many reasons, and not least among them the difficulty of deciding what is Christian and what pagan among later Egyptian productions, it is simpler to use the term to describe the style typical of the cult of Christian Egypt, even when the objects produced in that style are obviously pagan.

One would expect to find a large selection of Christian subjects among the earliest productions of Coptic art, for by the fourth and fifth centuries Christianity certainly dominated Egypt. But this is not the case. With rare exceptions Christian subjects are not found in objects produced in Egypt before the fifth century, and even then there is a very limited range of subjects. The earliest Christian objects from Egypt, mainly reliefs, usually depict a cross or saint in an Hellenistic or pagan setting.

This slow development of a purely Christian art was probably due to the Greek culture which had been the basis of education in Egypt for so many centuries. Greek had completely replaced Egyptian as the language of the educated man, and even Coptic, the latest form of the ancient Egyptian language, was written in Greek characters. A survey of the tattered books found in the town dumps of the period shows the vast majority of them to be standard Greek classics. The educated Egyptian Christian instinctively retained the cultural background of paganism, for which Christianity was slow in developing a substitute.

This new art of the Copts at first continued the Greek tradition, and Greek or Hellenistic subjects, particularly those from the Greek myths, are common. It is an art of limited range and, with the exception of architecture, it produced no monumental achievements. Nor did it even influence any other culture. Yet it achieved an unmistakable individuality, producing objects of outstanding beauty. At first glance Coptic art seems strange, even crude, but once the visitor understands that the Copts were not attempting realistic representations but were expressing their art in highly conventionalized terms, he will begin to realize the beauty of their achievements. Figures are usually sharply outlined, frontal, and depicted as if flat. In place of modelling we find sharp contrasts of colour. If several figures are depicted, each one is usually treated as a separate composition. Most compositions are conceived as designs employed to cover a surface. It is an art that has much in common with Byzantine art. Strangely, it shows almost no trace of ancient Egyptian influence.

Early Coptic sculpture retains some of the characteristics of the Roman period. The tendency towards division into local schools continues. Hellenistic or pagan subjects predominate. Sculpture in the round is almost nonexistent. But, we begin to find a unity of style in the relief sculpture of the fifth century.

Among the earliest, and unquestionably the greatest Coptic reliefs, are those coming from Ahnas, at the southeastern edge of the Faiyûm. Here, at about the beginning of the fifth century, arose a school which, during perhaps a century, produced sculpture of a very individual style. With a few important exceptions they are pagan in subject; but, pagan or Christian, the technique and treatment are alike. The fragment of relief from the top of a niche shown in Pl. 15 is said to be from Ahnas and is indeed typical of that school. The figures are in very high relief, so high that it is more logical to call them sculptures against a background. The plain background is a survival from Greek art that was not to linger long in Coptic Egypt. The acanthus border (not visible in the illustration) on this relief and also that on the relief in Pl. 17, which may have been influenced by the school of Ahnas, are Hellenistic survivals, as are some of the details of the figures. These sculptures are important, however, not as illustrations of the survival of Greek influence, but as early examples of figure sculpture embodying most of the characteristics of Coptic art.

In common with most Coptic art, these reliefs seem to have had only a decorative function, for the Copts apparently were not interested in expressing ideas through their art. The bodies are small and highly conventionalized, the heads enormous, with startlingly large eyes. In the Ahnas relief, the peculiar treatment of the eyes, which slope in sharply towards the cheeks, is probably due to the placing of the relief. Like most Coptic reliefs it was set well above eye level, and some convention had to be evolved to give the spectator the impression of direct connection with the sculpture. The result, an almost childish intensity of concentration, one could call it "playing to the gallery," is characteristic of Coptic art in general. In most figural compositions, whether in sculpture, painting or textiles, there is rarely any direct connection between the personages involved. They are always actors playing, not to each other, but to the audience. The action, frequently trivial, is handled decoratively, It matters little whether the Nereid's journey on the crocodile (Pl. 17) is interrupted, for she is probably not bound for any particular place. Nor are the animals in Pl. 21 engaged in anything more than a pleasant romp. Even in purely Christian reliefs, as those in Pls. 19 and 20, the saints have an eye on the spectator. Coptic art, unlike the art of ancient Egypt, has little to say and must be enjoyed for its technical and emotional qualities.

Its technical achievements are particularly noticeable in another important class of relief sculptures, the friezes or architectural decorations, numerous and at their best in the fifth and sixth centuries. It is perhaps in this field that Coptic sculpture found its most typical expression, for it is primarily a decorative art. Many motifs are found on these reliefs, but most important and frequent are the geometric, acanthus and, above all, the grapevine designs. Within the narrow bounds of these three groups the Copts developed endless variations, frequently incorporating with them human or animal figures. The relief in Pl. 14 is an example of the best Coptic architectural sculpture. Its workmanship will stand comparison with the finest Hellenistic work. Possibly embodying Christian symbolism, it is one of those works of art, all too rare, so direct that it can be enjoyed as deeply by the novice as by the expert. Unlike later Coptic sculpture, this relief abounds in motion. The heavy branches form roundels swirling in opposite directions, and the stems and leaves burst from the branches like sprays of water. The illusion of movement is increased by the very deep cutting, a technique common in Coptic reliefs, and sometimes enhanced by the use of color on the background. Most of these architectural reliefs come from Christian churches.

In the later sixth and seventh centuries a great change is noticeable in sculpture and in Coptic art in general. Hellenistic or pagan subjects disappear, and reliefs become very flat; they are sometimes little more than deeply incised designs. Backgrounds are filled with ornate designs, usually having no relation to the subject. Modelling disappears entirely from painting and sculpture, and a massive and static style comes in vogue. Harsh, and frequently muddy, colors replace the clear tones of the earlier centuries. Traces of these changes are evident in the sixth century reliefs in Pls. 19 and 20. Perhaps this was the logical culmination for a decorative art which relied on color more than on form for its effects. But some authorities ascribe these changes to Syrian influence, and there is certainly a marked Oriental feeling in the ornate backgrounds and the flat and formal treatment of late Coptic reliefs.

A selection from the Museum's collection of Coptic textiles is displayed in the gallery. The dry climate of Egypt has preserved a large group of this important field of Coptic art. It is hardly an exaggeration to claim that a complete history of Coptic design, covering the fields of stone, wood, ivory, bronze, etc., could be written from the patterns on these textiles, for they follow, both in style and subject, the trends indicated above for sculpture and Coptic art in general. This is striking evidence of the unity of the art developed by the Christian Egyptians after so many centuries of conflicting influences.

The early fragment in Pl. 41 could be a copy of the decoration of a Roman pilaster; it is almost purely Hellenistic and gives a distinct feeling of depth. Contrast this with the later border of praying persons in Pl. 47, where the pattern is flat, the personages increasingly conventionalized and sharply outlined, and each section of the design is a separate unit complete in itself. In these two pieces — and others would serve equally well — we can clearly trace the development of Coptic art.

One of the commonest motifs of the textiles is the series of roundels or connected medallions enclosing animals or floral motifs. These are particularly frequent in the fifth and earlier sixth centuries and should be compared with the same design in stone. As in stonework, Christian subjects are rare, but a few Christian pieces from Antinoë are exhibited. Attempts have been made, so far without success, to read a Christian symbolism into Coptic usage of pagan myths.

13

Most of the fabrics shown are fragments from large hangings used in churches and homes, or from garments. The great majority of these are linen with tapestry-woven ornament in wool. All-wool textiles are far less common and usually late, and cotton is found only very exceptionally and then always in combination with other fibres. Few unquestionably Egyptian silks have survived. While certain textiles were almost certainly imported into Egypt, and others, such as the square in Pl. 41, were probably Egyptian copies of Oriental patterns, the bulk of the fabrics are of Egyptian origin. The illustrations give no hint of the rich colors of these textiles, which are at their best in those pieces with subjects taken from Greek sources. The later textiles are less attractive in color, and their occasionally startling combination of colors reflects the Oriental cast of later Coptic culture.

Coptic art of the later sixth and seventh centuries never equalled the achievements attained under the Greek tradition. Perhaps it is not fair to judge it, for the Arab conquest of Egypt early in the seventh century impoverished the Coptic church and smothered the development of the later type of Coptic art. The marked decline both in design and technique after the late sixth century does not favor a prediction of new achievements, even had conditions remained favorable. Under Arabic influence Coptic art produced, during the medieval period, many fine objects affording an interesting study of Christian art in a Moslem country. A very few of these objects are exhibited, but they belong to another chapter in the long history of Egypt.

JOHN D. COONEY*

* Most of the copy for this Handbook had been prepared by Mr. Cooney before he was called into the Service in April, 1942. He wrote the Introduction after his induction, during the brief leisure permitted by his Army duties. He has not been able, however, to make additions or corrections, nor to revise the proofs of this publication. THE EDITOR

# NOTES TO THE PLATES

FOR the convenience of those who wish to use for study the illustrations here reproduced, remarks and bibliographies have been included on the following pages. The reference *P.C.E.* refers to the catalogue, *Pagan and Christian Egypt,* published by the Brooklyn Museum Press for the Exhibition of Coptic Art held at the Brooklyn Museum in 1941. Bibliographies given in *P.C.E.* are not repeated here. That catalogue is out of print, but is available in most libraries.

**PLATE 1.** Portrait of Demetris. Encaustic on cypress panel. Probably painted from life when Demetris was about fifty and placed on the mummy when Demetris died at the age of eighty-nine. From the Roman cemetery at Hawara.

| | | | |
|---|---|---|---|
| *Graeco-Egyptian* | *First half of IInd century* | *P.C.E. No. 2* | *H. 37.3 cm.* |
| | *Museum Collection Fund* | | |

**PLATE 2.** Portrait of a man. Encaustic on cypress panel. Certainly a life-portrait. The gold wreath, a pagan symbol comparable to the halo, was probably added when the painting was inserted in the mummy wrappings.

| | | | |
|---|---|---|---|
| *Graeco-Egyptian* | *Second half of IInd century* | *P.C.E. No. 3* | *H. 36 cm.* |
| | *Charles Edwin Wilbour Fund* | | |

**PLATE 3.** Tempera portrait on cypress panel. Mr. William C. Darrah of Harvard University has very kindly identified the wood of this panel as well as that of the two preceding panels as *cupressus sempervirens*, a common evergreen tree. No. 9 of the Graf collection. See Graf, Theodor, *Catalogue of Theodor Graf's Gallery of Antique Portraits of the Hellenistic Period*, Berlin, 1899, No. 9. Also listed as No. 9 in subsequent publications of this work, including the revised catalogue of Buberl, P., *Die griechisch-ägyptischen Mumienbildnisse der Sammlung Th. Graf*, Wien, 1922, p. 51. From Er-Rubiyât in the Faiyûm (Graf's statement. See also Baedeker's *Egypt*, Leipzig, 1929, p. 204). For a parallel piece, cf. Galerie Georges Petit, *Collection du Dr. Fouquet, du Caire* [Sale catalogue], June, 1922, pte. II, pl. I, No. 104. For possible interpretation of garland in left hand, cf. Wilpert, J., *Die Malereien der Katakomben Roms*, Freiburg, 1903, p. 34, 37, pls. 86, 87, 91, 95-97, etc.

| | | | |
|---|---|---|---|
| *Coptic* | *IVth century* | *P.C.E. No. 6* | *H. 30.2 cm.* |
| | *Charles Edwin Wilbour Fund* | | |

**PLATE 4.** Life-size painted plaster mask of a man, from a coffin or cartonnage. Inlaid eyes of opaque white glass, with dark brown opaque glass pupils. Painted black eyebrows. Modelled beard on cheeks and on chin. Hair at forehead modelled in long wavy locks, on top of head in short curls. Flesh painted pale pink. The treatment of hair and beard, together with the use of opaque glass inlay for eyes, points to time of Hadrian and Antoninus Pius (138-161 A.D.). For dating and related examples, cf. Edgar, C. C., *Graeco-Egyptian Coffins, Masks, and Portraits* (Catalogue général, Musée du Caire), Cairo, 1905.

| | | |
|---|---|---|
| *Graeco-Roman* | *IInd century* | *H. about 24 cm.* |
| | *Bought in Egypt for the Brooklyn Museum by Sir W. M. F. Petrie* | |
| | *Museum Collection Fund* | |

**PLATES 5-6.** Marble head of Zeus with ram's horns of the god Amon. The stone is not Egyptian. Many similar pieces are extant in stone and terra-cotta (e.g. Edgar, C. C., *Greek Sculpture* <Catalogue général, Musée du Caire>, Cairo, 1903, pl. II). They are probably based on the famous statue of Sarapis by Bryaxis. As seems to have been customary in Graeco-Egyptian work, the head was made as a separate piece.

*Alexandrian*                  *Late IInd century B.C.*                  *H. 26 cm.*
*Anderson Collection*
*From the Collections of the New York Historical Society in the Brooklyn Museum*

**PLATE 7.** Female face and neck in Pentelic marble (the goddess Venus?). Apparently made as a separate piece. Traces of orange-red paint on lips, hair and eyes; the latter were also outlined in black. The slightly tilted head seems to be characteristic of Alexandrian work. Cf. the similar colossal head published by Edgar in *Greek Sculpture*, No. 27468, pl. X.

*Alexandrian*              *After an original of the IIIrd century B.C.*              *H. 21 cm.*
*Charles Edwin Wilbour Collection*

**PLATE 8.** Painted limestone sphinx with human head and beard, wearing the *nemes* headdress, probably formerly surmounted by a crown, and a short apron-like garment, on the lower edge of which is a small lion's (?) head in relief. Legs rest on uraeus serpents and tail ends in uraeus: Central support under belly with painted Bes head in relief on one side; on the other a painted griffon. Crudely modelled crocodile between front paws. Small animal head (jackal?) in relief on back at base of headdress. Abundant remains of red and black paint. A pantheistic deity of late times, perhaps the demi-god Tithoës. Mentioned in *Catalogue of a Collection of Egyptian Antiquities, the Property of Henry Abbott, Esq., M.D.*, Cairo, 1846, p. 4, no. 37, where it is said to come from Saqqâra. For a close parallel in the United States National Museum, see *Annual Report of the Smithsonian Institution*, Washington, 1922, p. 462, pl. 25-26. For a discussion of the symbolism, see Mallon, Alexis, Basreliefs du Sphinx, in *Revue archéologique*, 4. sér., t. V, 1905, p. 169 ff. Also Guéraud, Octave, Sphinx composites au Musée du Caire, in *Annales du Service des Antiquités de l'Égypte*, t. XXXV, p. 4 ff., and Seyrig, Henri, Tithoës, Totoës et le Sphinx panthée, in the same volume, p. 197 ff. For a painted representation of a similar sphinx from about the IIIrd century, see Boak, A. E. R., and Peterson, E. E., *Karanis . . . 1924-28*, Ann Arbor, 1931 (Univ. of Mich. Studies, Humanistic Series, v. XXV), p. 56, fig. 71.

*Graeco-Roman*                  *About IInd century*                  *H. 37.5 cm., l. 42 cm.*
*Abbott Collection*
*From the Collections of the New York Historical Society in the Brooklyn Museum*

**PLATE 9.** Black basalt bust of a man carrying a ram on his shoulders. The reign of Trajan seems to be the latest possible date, unless this is an archaistic work of a later period. The significance is unknown. For similar examples cf. Weber, W., *Die ägyptisch-griechischen Terrakotten*, Berlin, 1914, pl. 28, No. 294-295; Petrie, Sir W. M. F., *Roman Ehnasya*, London, 1905, pl. XLV, No. 11; *Encyclopédie photographique de l'art*, Paris, 1936, t. II, p. 121, d; Cabrol and Leclercq, *Dictionnaire d'archéologie chrétienne*, Paris, 1914, t. III, pte. 2, p. 1675, fig. 2950.

*Egypto-Roman*          *Probably early IInd century*          *P.C.E. No. 18*          *H. 23.5 cm.*
*Abbott Collection*
*From the Collections of the New York Historical Society in the Brooklyn Museum*

**PLATE 10.** Marble portrait head. Roman work from Egypt. Its use is not apparent. The base is smooth and the object is complete. Compare the similar, undated (but probably also Constantinian) specimen published by Edgar, C. C., *Greek Bronzes* (Catalogue général, Musée du Caire), pl. V, no. 27711. The type may be peculiar to Egypt.

*Roman*                        *Early IVth century*                        H. 10.5 cm.
                        *Charles Edwin Wilbour Collection*

**PLATE 11.** Tombstone of a Roman boy. Limestone. He makes an offering on a small altar surrounded by Egyptian and Greek deities.

*Egypto-Roman*              *IIIrd century*          *P.C.E. No. 33*          H. 35.7 cm., w. 25.8 cm.
                        *Charles Edwin Wilbour Collection*

**PLATE 12.** Tombstone of Chairemon, a Greek resident of Egypt. He stands with uplifted arms, the Greek attitude of prayer (orans). At his feet are jackals, sacred to the Egyptian god of the dead, Anubis.

*Graeco-Egyptian*          *IVth (?) century*          *P.C.E. No. 35*          H. 38.9 cm., w. 33.5 cm.
                        *Charles Edwin Wilbour Collection*

**PLATE 13.** Tombstone of Olympios. Limestone, with remains of red paint. He stands within a shrine crowning himself with a laurel wreath, the pagan symbol of a beatified deceased. Cf. *The Art Bulletin*, v. XXIII, June, 1941, p. 166.

*Coptic*              *Vth century*              *P.C.E. No. 36*              H. 37.8 cm., w. 29 cm.
                        *Charles Edwin Wilbour Fund*

**PLATE 14.** Limestone frieze with animals in acanthus scrolls. From left to right the animals represented are a wild boar, gazelle, hyena, dog and leopard. There are numerous drill holes on the background and some portions of the scrolls are completely in the round.

*Coptic*              *Vth century*              *P.C.E. No. 40*              H. 35.5 cm., w. 128 cm.
                        *Acquired by exchange with the University Museum, Philadelphia*

**PLATES 15-16.** Reclining river god (Nile?) and the Earth goddess among lotus flowers. Fragment of a large relief from the top of a niche in compact limestone, probably symbolizing land and water. A delicate vine design borders the upper edge of the niche. This does not show in the illustration, as the relief has been mounted vertically for exhibition. The peculiar treatment of the eyes in this relief (they slope in sharply from the eyebrow toward the cheek) is probably a technical device used because of the great height at which the sculpture was originally placed. Similar treatments, including the use of elongated eyes, are found in colossal sculptures of the New Kingdom in Egypt. Said to be from Ahnas. For similar types, cf. Monneret de Villard, Ugo, *La Scultura ad Ahnas*, Milano, 1923, figs. 8, 9 and 16. For the dating and an excellent discussion of the school of Ahnas, cf. Kitzinger, Ernst, Notes on Early Coptic Sculpture, in *Archaeologia*, v. 87, Oxford, 1937, p. 181 ff.

*Coptic*              *Second half of Vth century*              H. 38.5 cm., w. 64.5 cm.
                        *Charles Edwin Wilbour Fund*

**PLATES 17-18.** Nereid on crocodile. Relief from the top of a niche in soft limestone with remains of orange-red and black paint. A decorative subject frequently found in Nilotic scenes on textiles. Plain background. The border is similar to the floral wreath in Plate 3. Provenance unknown, but possibly influenced by the school of Ahnas. Acquired in Egypt

c. 1900 by the French collector, Count Sursok, it entered in 1926 an American private collection, from which it recently came to the Museum.

Coptic                    Vth — early VIth (?) century                    H. 46 cm., w. 80 cm., depth 39 cm.
                          Charles Edwin Wilbour Fund

**PLATE 19.** Relief of St. Sisinnios. Soft limestone. The elaborate background and the flatness of the relief are typical of later Coptic sculpture. For another interpretation of this subject, cf. *The Art Bulletin*, v. XXIII, June 1941, p. 166.

Coptic            VIth century              P.C.E. No. 58              H. 38.3 cm., w. 58 cm.
                          Charles Edwin Wilbour Fund

**PLATE 20.** Martyrdom of St. Thekla. Soft limestone. A favorite subject in Coptic art and literature.

Coptic            VIth century              P.C.E. No. 59              H. 33.5 cm., w. 58.3 cm.
                          Charles Edwin Wilbour Fund

**PLATE 21.** Lion attacking gazelle. Soft limestone with conventionalized grapevine background. The subject is common in Coptic art but probably has no iconographic meaning.

Coptic            VIth century              P.C.E. No. 60              H. 20.5 cm., w. 53 cm.
                          Charles Edwin Wilbour Fund

**PLATE 22.** Left: Small wooden door, perhaps from a shrine, with a saint, orans, in relief. Iron lock.

Coptic            VIIth century             P.C.E. No. 71              H. 16.1 cm., w. 14.8 cm.
                          The Gift of Mrs. R. T. Costantino

Right: Wooden inlay of a saint.

Coptic      Period uncertain but possibly early Arabic      P.C.E. No. 70      H. 21.8 cm., w. 8.5 cm.
                          The Gift of Mrs. R. T. Costantino

**PLATE 23.** Bronze statuette of Isis wearing archaistic Greek chiton. Cast hollow. The metal is of poor quality with a high proportion of lead, probably to facilitate the casting. The arms and headdress were cast solid, separately. Eyes originally inlaid. A well-known type. Cf. Edgar, *Greek Bronzes*, Nos. 27669-27673.

Graeco-Egyptian              Probably Ist century              H. 36.6 cm.
                          Museum Collection Fund

**PLATE 24.** Bronze statuette of Hathor-Aphrodite, the Egyptian and Greek goddesses of love. Represented dancing (?). Cast hollow in one piece with eyes inlaid in black and white glass. An excellent specimen of debased Alexandrian work with Egyptian details. The hands probably held objects (castanets?) now missing. Cf. Erman, A., *A Handbook of Egyptian Religion*, London, 1907, p. 218.

Graeco-Egyptian              Ist-IIIrd century              H. 32 cm.
                          Abbott Collection
            From the Collections of the New York Historical Society in the Brooklyn Museum

**PLATES 25-26.** Bronze statuette of Hercules. Said to be from Alexandria. Cast solid in three parts. The stylization of the face and body of this familiar classical subject shows the general trend, not only of Egyptian work but of Mediterranean art in general. To be published by Prof. Lehmann-Hartleben.

Roman            IIIrd century              P.C.E. No. 80              H. 31.2 cm.
                          Museum Collection Fund

18

**PLATES 27-28.** Bronze altar cast in sections, from Tell el-Yahûdîya in the Delta. Base lost. Central support with four spirally fluted columns supporting square top with high sides and flaring corners. In center of each side a uraeus within aedicula flanked on two sides by busts of Isis and Sarapis and on the other two by male masks. The stationary rings below the masks are probably not for suspension. Lion masks with movable rings in the mouths are on a similar unpublished piece in Brooklyn and they could not bear the weight of the object.

These altars are frequently called "fire altars" but they do not seem to have any connection with Persia. A comparable altar in stone is illustrated in Boak, A. E. R., ed., *Karanis* (Seasons 1924-31. Univ. of Mich. Studies. Humanistic Series, v. XXX), Ann Arbor, 1933, p. 10 ff., pl. VII, figs. 14-15.

*Egypto-Roman*                     *IIIrd-IVth (?) century*                     *Present H. 22.5 cm.*
*Abbott Collection*
*From the Collections of the New York Historical Society in the Brooklyn Museum*

**PLATE 29.** Bronze altar with square base resting on four low feet. Cast in one piece with hollow column. Top has flaring corners terminating in round knobs. From Egypt and probably of native manufacture; but cf. Rostovtzeff, *The Excavations at Dura-Europas* (Fifth Season), New Haven, 1934, p. 49, pl. XXIII, where the type is called Parthian. As Edgar shows in *Greek Bronzes*, pl. XV, No. 27810, a very similar altar presumably from Egypt, it seems safe to infer that the type was common both to Egypt and the Near East.

*IInd-IIIrd century*                                         *H. 11.5 cm., base 7.3 cm. square*
*Abbott Collection*
*From the Collections of the New York Historical Society in the Brooklyn Museum*

**PLATE 30.**  Above: Ivory inlay with naturalistic grapevine in relief.
*Coptic*                              *IV-Vth century*                          *12.4 x 4 cm.*
*Abbott Collection*
*From the Collections of the New York Historical Society in the Brooklyn Museum*
Below: Bronze lamp, originally with cover. Handle a cross within circle surmounted by duck.
*Coptic*          *Vth-VIth century*          *P.C.E. No. 83*          *H. 8.6 cm., w. 7.5 cm.*
*Charles Edwin Wilbour Collection*

**PLATES 31-32.** Bronze incense burner. Rim of conventionalized ducks on rings. Greek inscription on exterior of bowl. Probably a church vessel. Cast in three sections.
*Coptic*          *About Vth century*          *P.C.E. No. 85*          *H. 28.5 cm., diam. of bowl, 13.8 cm.*
*Charles Edwin Wilbour Fund*

**PLATE 33.** Bronze lamp on pricket stand. A typical specimen of a well-known type, probably for church use.
*Coptic*                              *About the VIth century*                          *H. 37.9 cm.*
*Charles Edwin Wilbour Fund*

**PLATE 34.** Bronze censer showing, in high relief, scenes from the life of Christ. The type seems to have been common to Syria and Egypt, but several specimens, including this one, can be traced to the art trade in Cairo, making an Egyptian provenance probable. The censer was cast in one piece and the details of the figures cut after casting, the eyes being made with a hollow cylindrical tool. Compare the border on the neck with the very similar treatment of the same pattern in the leaves of the upper textile pl. 40, and the border of the lower textile pl. 44. A cross of a well-known Coptic type is present in the Annunciation scene on

19

this censer. For discussion of the type and reference to most published specimens, cf. *Archäologischer Anzeiger, Beiblatt zum Jahrbuch des Deutschen archäologischen Instituts,* bd. 55, 1940, p. 62-63, fig. 55-60.

*Coptic*     *VIth-VIIIth century*        *P.C.E. No.* 91          *H.* 13 *cm., w.* 10.8 *cm.*
*Charles Edwin Wilbour Fund*

**PLATE 35.** Painted terra-cotta female figurines. A well-known Coptic type of uncertain use. Possibly funerary figurines.

*Coptic*     *VIth-VIIth century*        *P.C.E. Nos.* 126-127       *H.* 13.4 *cm. and* 14.5 *cm.*
*Charles Edwin Wilbour Collection*

**PLATE 36.** Large pottery dish with fish decoration. Heavy, coarse ware. The body, of reddish clay, on moderately high hollow foot, is united by a slightly concave band to a wide, flat rim. The center apparently once contained a shallow, bowl-shaped depression, with raised, molded edge, now broken away. Pale orange slip with traces of whitish slip at rim and on outside. Rim pierced with eight small holes (piercings modern?). Decoration on outer rim and around central depression of guilloche in black with blobs of red on white (?) slip. Undulated line with blobs (degenerated vine pattern) on concave part joining bowl with rim. Body decorated with four flat fish (*telopia nilotica*) outlined in black with splash of red in each scale. Long before the Christian era, the fish was used as an amulet; it became a symbol of Christianity and finally of Christ, the letters of the Greek word for fish forming an acrostic for the Greek phrase meaning "Jesus Christ, Son of God, Savior." For another compartment-plate but with five compartments see Winlock, *The Monastery of Epiphanius at Thebes* (Metropolitan Museum of Art. Egyptian Expedition. Publications), New York, 1926, pl. XXXIII, which also shows plate with fish decoration. Other pottery with fish decoration in *Fouilles Franco-Polonaise, Rapports II, Tell Edfou, 1938,* Cairo, 1938, p. 23-24, pl. XXVIII. For discussion of fish as Christian symbol see article "Ichthus" in Cabrol and Leclercq, *Dictionnaire d'archéologie chrétienne,* t. VII, pte. 2, Paris, 1927, p. 1990-2086.

*Coptic*     *VIth century*      *P.C.E. No.* 124      *H.* 11.3 *cm., diam.* 47.5 *cm., thickness at rim* 1.3 *cm.*
*Charles Edwin Wilbour Fund*

**PLATE 37.** Oblong black steatite mould for two circular amulets with suspension loops. Obverse, negative of conventionalized crucifixion showing bust of Christ with cruciferous nimbus flanked by nimbed thieves (?). Reverse with negative of square cross.

The mould originally included three parts, the piece illustrated, and two flat pieces of corresponding size each with keys that were inserted in the holes on the diagonally opposite corners of the negatives. The metal was poured into the channels at the top. A rod, run through the horizontal grooves seen above the negatives, provided for the opening in the loop and was removed after casting. The mould is identical in material and form with jewelry moulds of the Roman period in Egypt. The dating is uncertain. While the cross is of an early type, the angular style of the crucifixion figures suggests a date after the fifth century. There is some similarity of style with a limited group of textiles, a typical example of which is illustrated in *P.C.E. No.* 260.

For a casting from an almost identical mould, cf. Wulff, O., and Volbach, W. F., *Die altchristlichen und mittelalterlichen byzantinischen und italienischen Bildwerke,* Berlin, 1923, bd. 3, p. 45, nr. J6726; or discussion of same piece by Wulff, in the *Amtliche Berichte* of the Berlin Museum, v. XXXV, p. 43.

*Coptic*     *VIth-VIIth century*        *P.C.E. No.* 143          *H.* 7.3 *cm., w.* 3.9 *cm.*
*Charles Edwin Wilbour Collection*

**PLATE 38.** Left: Purple wool square with design of geometric interlacing in undyed linen thread.

In this and the following descriptions of textiles the first dimension given is that of direction of the weft.

*Coptic*          *IIIrd-IVth century*          *P.C.E. No.* 145          39.7 x 33 *cm.*
*The Gift of the Long Island Historical Society*

Right: Purple wool square with design of geometric interlacing in undyed linen thread.

*Coptic*          *IIIrd-IVth century*          *P.C.E. No.* 146          37.5 x 37 *cm.*
*Abbott Collection*
*From the Collections of the New York Historical Society in the Brooklyn Museum*


**PLATE 39.** Above: Dancing figures within arches. Design in purple wool on undyed linen.

*Coptic*          *IVth-Vth century*          *P.C.E. No.* 191          18.5 x 34 *cm.*
*The Gift of Pratt Institute*

Lower left: Square with amorino and dolphin in purple wool on undyed linen.

*Coptic*          *IVth-Vth century*          *P.C.E. No.* 190          12 *cm. square*
*The Gift of Pratt Institute*

Lower right: Detail from (probably) a series of borders now assembled. Small squares each containing portrait head, bird or floral detail.

*Coptic*          *VIth century*          *P.C.E. No.* 225          24 x 16 *cm. (complete textile)*
*The Gift of Pratt Institute*


**PLATE 40.** Above: Wool and linen textile with vine growing in urn. Vine deep blue, urn and fruit red.

*Coptic*          *IVth-Vth century*          *P.C.E. No.* 157          21.5 x 16.5 *cm.*
*Permanent loan from Pratt Institute*

Lower left: Wool and linen square with purple hare under red and green foliage.

*Coptic*          *IVth-Vth century*          *P.C.E. No.* 159          21 *cm. square*
*Permanent loan from Pratt Institute*

Lower right: Haloed head within oblong. Borders with Nilotic scenes. Undyed linen background. Blue halo. Head, dark blue and red. Details in green, red and blue.

*Coptic*          *VIth century*          *P.C.E. No.* 220          24 *cm. square*
*Permanent loan from Pratt Institute*


**PLATE 41.** Left: Tapestry-woven border with conventionalized grapevine in purple wool and undyed linen. One of the commonest Coptic motifs found in every medium. Cf. the similar treatment in the VIth century relief in *Bulletin de l'Association des Amis de l'Art copte*, t. III, Cairo, 1937, pl. II, fig. 4.

*Coptic*          *IVth-Vth century*          *P.C.E. No.* 158          48.5 x 8.9 *cm.*
*The Gift of Pratt Institute*

Upper right: Fragment with jewelled cross. Cross with polychromed "jewels" on red ground, set into undyed linen.

*Coptic*          *Vth-VIth century*          *P.C.E. No.* 247          14.5 x 16 *cm.*
*The Gift of Pratt Institute*

Lower right: Square in black wool and undyed linen divided into four compartments. The design is probably not of Egyptian origin.

*Coptic*          *VIth-VIIth century*          *P.C.E. No.* 173          14.5 *cm. square*
*The Gift of Pratt Institute*

**PLATE 42.** Border with haloed heads. Brilliant polychromy on dark blue background. Very similar friezes are found in church frescoes although this textile is probably pagan.

*Coptic*          *IVth century*          *P.C.E. No. 185*          *57 x 18 cm.*
*Charles Edwin Wilbour Fund*

**PLATE 43.** Winged genius with fruit basket. A Hellenistic design in looped technique.

*Coptic*          *IVth-Vth century*          *P.C.E. No. 236*          *37 x 30 cm.*
*Charles Edwin Wilbour Fund*

**PLATE 44.** Top: Detail of tapestry-woven band set in looped fabric, probably a hanging. Series of black roundels enclosing black animals with red tongues. Floral details in green, red, yellow and black. From Akhmîm. See *The De Potter Collection* (n.p., n.d.) A 259.

*Coptic*          *Vth century*          *59 x 35 cm. (complete textile)*
*Museum Collection Fund*

Center: Band with acanthus design enclosing animals and birds. Purple-red wool on undyed linen.

*Coptic*          *IVth-Vth century*          *P.C.E. No. 160*          *43 x 7.5 cm.*
*The Gift of Pratt Institute*

Bottom: Band with roundels enclosing plants and animals. Red wool background and details in brilliant colors.

*Coptic*          *VIIth century*          *P.C.E. No. 180*          *42 x 8.5 cm.*
*The Gift of Pratt Institute*

**PLATE 45.** Top: Wool and linen strip. Rose-red background with conventionalized floral design in undyed linen thread enclosing animals and portraits in medallions. Pomegranate border.

*Coptic*          *Vth-VIth century*          *30.4 x 6.1 cm.*
*The Gift of Pratt Institute*

Bottom: Tapestry-woven band. From a woolen tunic. Borders and roundels in black enclosing animals and figures in black and red.

*Coptic*          *VIth century*          *P.C.E. No. 172*          *84 x 16 cm.*
*Charles Edwin Wilbour Fund*

**PLATE 46.** Textiles from Antinoë.

Upper left: Roundel with acrostic, reading horizontally "life" and vertically "light."

*Coptic*          *Vth-VIth century*          *P.C.E. No. 245*          *Diam. 3.2 cm.*

Lower left: Roundel with Pasiphae (?) and the Bull. Rose-red background. Yellow, green and natural linen details.

*Coptic*          *Vth-VIth century*          *P.C.E. No. 215*          *Diam. 10 cm.*

Center: Fragment of border from tunic of fine green wool. Lozenges enclosing human figures in purple wool on white linen background. Floral details and borders in purple. Very fine weave.

*Coptic*          *Vth-VIth century*          *32 x 8 cm.*

Upper right: Stag, probably symbolizing Christ, outlined in blue. Flowers in red, green and blue. Wool, undyed linen and cotton (?).

*Coptic*          *Vth-VIth century*          *P.C.E. No. 246*          *5.5 x 5.5 cm.*

Lower right: Tapestry-woven cross in brown and gold. Design in silk and linen on silk warp and linen weft.

*Coptic*          *Vth-VIth century*          *P.C.E. No. 244*          *4 x 4.5 cm.*
*All specimens gift of Col. Robert B. Woodward from the excavations of the*
*Egypt Exploration Society at Antinoë, 1913-14*

**PLATE 47.** Left: Detail of border with roundels containing, alternatingly, a rosette and an orans. Purple wool and undyed linen.

*Coptic*               *Vth–VIth century*               *P.C.E. No. 248*               *50 x 10.5 cm.*
*The Gift of Pratt Institute*

Right: Band with heart-shaped leaves. Vine in purple on white ground.

*Coptic*               *IVth–Vth century*               *P.C.E. No. 156*               *49.5 x 24 cm.*
*The Gift of Pratt Institute*

**PLATE 48.** Front of tunic. Yellow wool with borders of nymphs and sea-monsters on brown background.

*Coptic*               *Late VIth century*               *P.C.E. No. 255*               *113 x 33 cm.*
*Charles Edwin Wilbour Fund*

**PLATES 49-50.** Coptic tunic of yellow wool rep with tapestry-woven bands in dark blue and pale purple wool and white linen thread. The garment, not including the sleeves, is almost square. It is very slightly shaped, tapering out at the waist line. A broad tuck at the waist formerly held a girdle cord. The tunic is slit at the sides to the waist and finished along the slit, as at the wrists, with a yellow wool cord. A fringe at the lower edge of the tunic is almost completely preserved. The sleeves are slit almost to the arm-hole, and indications are that they were never sewn. The usual long-sleeved tunic as shown, for instance, at Bawît, has the sleeves fitted tightly to the lower arm and wrist, and the extra width of the very wide garment falls over the tight sleeve in rich folds. Experiments on a living model suggest that the open sleeves of this tunic fell over the hand.

While it seems improbable that the tunic can be earlier than the VIIth century, greatly degenerated classical designs still survive in the ornament—figures standing by columns, urns with conventionalized fruits. Other subjects are suggestive of the Nilotic scenes, so frequent in Coptic textiles, and one roundel shows a horseman in a Phrygian cap. Most interesting of all, however, is the band across the front of the tunic (pl. 50), which shows a figure between two fantastic animals with long beaks, which might be interpreted, in the light of old legend, as Alexander carried to Heaven by the griffins.

*Coptic*          *VIIth century*          *P.C.E. No. 267*          L. 132 *cm., w. (not incl. sleeves)* 145 *cm.*
*Charles Edwin Wilbour Fund*

**PLATE 51.** Tapestry-woven square in wool and linen. Central roundel with female portrait bust. Outer border of roundels enclosing birds and animals. Red, blue, orange, yellow, purple and black. This textile, or a duplicate from the same manufacture, published in *Catalogue of the Collection of Egyptian Antiquities, Formed in Egypt by R. de Rustafjaell . . .* [Sale catalogue], Sotheby, London, 1906, pl. XXI, No. 13.

*Coptic*               *VIth century*               *33 x 37 cm.*
*Charles Edwin Wilbour Fund*

**PLATE 52.** Above: Wool and linen textile. The elements are ancient and possibly related, but have been assembled in modern times. Several similarly assembled pieces are known, all probably the work of the same modern Arab.

*Coptic*          *IVth–Vth century*          *P.C.E. No. 237*          *Diam. 50 cm.*
*The Gift of the Long Island Historical Society*

23

Lower left: Square with fruit basket. Green, red and black wool on linen. This textile, or a duplicate from the same manufacture, published in the sales catalogue of the de Rustafjaell collection (see note to pl. 51).

Coptic                  Vth century                  P.C.E. No. 163                  About 30 cm. square
                              Charles Edwin Wilbour Fund

Lower right: Roundel with haloed figure in a chariot. Wool with brown, red and green predominating.

Coptic                  VIth century                  P.C.E. No. 251                  Diam. 12 cm.
                              Museum Collection Fund


**PLATE 53.** Green woolen tunic-front. Applied tapestry-woven bands in brilliant colors with saints, animals and trees.

Coptic                  VIth century                  P.C.E. No. 254                  80 x 27 cm.
                              Charles Edwin Wilbour Fund


**PLATE 54.** Tapestry-woven fragments in wool and linen, of the early Arabic period.
Left: White lozenges against red background. Floral and animal designs in yellow, blue, green and black.

Coptic                  VIIth-VIIIth century                  11.5 x 38 cm.
                              Charles Edwin Wilbour Fund

Right: White lozenges against dark blue background. Birds and floral motifs in rose, yellow and blue. The type is discussed by Ernst Kühnel in *Bulletin de la Société d'Archéologie copte*, t. IV, Cairo, 1938, p. 79 ff., pl. I.

Coptic                  VIIth-VIIIth century                  13. 5 x 43 cm.
                              Charles Edwin Wilbour Fund


NOTE: The photographs from which these plates were made were produced by the Photography Studio of the Brooklyn Museum, under the supervision of Herman de Wetter.

PLATES

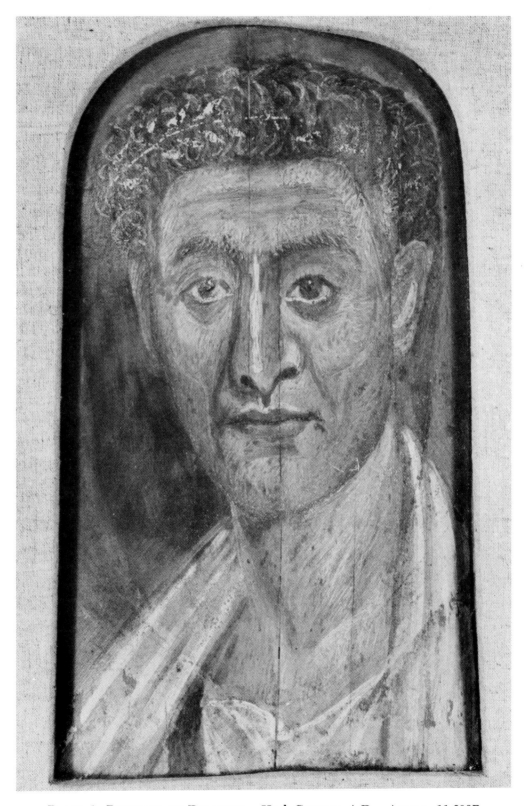

PLATE 1. PORTRAIT OF DEMETRIS — IInd Century A.D.   Acc.no. 11.600B

PLATE 2. PORTRAIT OF A MAN — IInd Century A.D.   Acc.no. 40.386

PLATE 3. FUNERARY PORTRAIT OF A BOY — IVth Century A.D.   Acc.no. 41.848

PLATE 4. LIFE-SIZE PAINTED PLASTER MASK OF A MAN — IInd Century A.D.
Acc.no. 05.392

PLATE 5. MARBLE HEAD OF ZEUS-AMON, ALEXANDRIAN — IInd Century B.C.
Acc.no. 37.1522E

PLATE 6. MARBLE HEAD OF ZEUS-AMON, ALEXANDRIAN — IInd Century B.C.
Acc.no. 37.1522E

PLATE 7. MARBLE HEAD OF VENUS (?), ALEXANDRIAN
Acc.no. 16.580.82

PLATE 8. PAINTED LIMESTONE FIGURE OF A SPHINX — IInd Century A.D.
Acc.no. 37.1509E

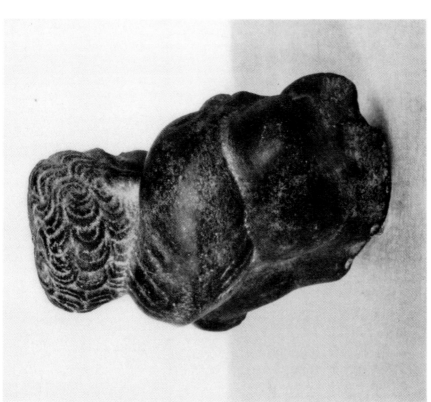

PLATE 9. MAN CARRYING RAM, BASALT — Ist-IInd Century A.D.    Acc.no.  37.1499E

PLATE 10. PORTRAIT HEAD, MARBLE — IVth Century A.D.   Acc.no. 16.239

PLATE 11. TOMBSTONE OF A ROMAN BOY — IIIrd Century A.D.   Acc.no. 16.105

PLATE 12. TOMBSTONE OF A GREEK NAMED CHAIREMON — IVth Century A.D.
Acc.no. 16.90

PLATE 13. TOMBSTONE OF OLYMPIOS, COPTIC — Vth Century A.D.   Acc.no. 40.301

PLATE 14. Limestone Relief with Animals in Acanthus Scrolls, Coptic – Vth Century A.D.
Acc.no. 41.1266

PLATE 15. RIVER GOD AND EARTH GODDESS, LIMESTONE – Vth Century A.D.   Acc.no. 41.891

PLATE 16. DETAIL OF RIVER GOD · Acc.no. 41.891

PLATE 17. NYMPH ON CROCODILE, LIMESTONE – Vth-VIth Century A.D.   Acc.no.  41.1226

PLATE 18. DETAIL OF NYMPH  Acc.no. 41.1226

PLATE 19. St. Sisinnios, Limestone – VIth Century A.D.   Acc.no.   40.300

PLATE 20. MARTYRDOM OF ST. THEKLA, LIMESTONE – VIth Century A.D.    Acc.no.  40.299

PLATE 21. LION ATTACKING GAZELLE, LIMESTONE – VIth Century A.D.   Acc.no. 40.302

PLATE 22. (LEFT) DOOR WITH PRAYING SAINT, COPTIC – VIITH CENTURY A.D.   ACC.NO. 30.28
(RIGHT) WOODEN INLAY OF A SAINT, COPTIC   ACC.NO. 30.27

PLATE 23. ISIS IN GREEK COSTUME, BRONZE — Ist Century A.D.
Acc.no. 05.395

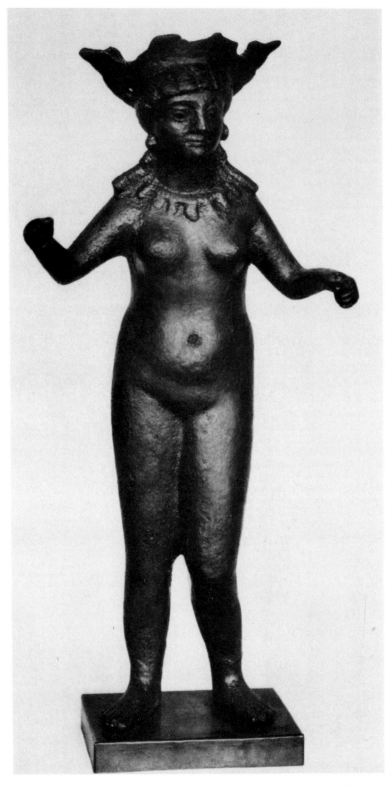

PLATE 24. VENUS-HATHOR, GODDESS OF LOVE, BRONZE — Ist-IIIrd Century A.D.
Acc.no. 37.572E

PLATE 25. HERCULES WITH LION SKIN — IIIrd Century A.D.
Acc.no. 36.161

PLATE 26. DETAIL OF HERCULES HEAD   ACC.NO. 36.161

PLATE 27. BRONZE ALTAR — IIIrd-IVth Century A.D.   Acc.no. 37.1614E

PLATE 28. DETAIL OF ALTAR, SHOWING BUSTS OF ISIS AND SERAPIS   ACC.NO. 36.1614E

PLATE 29. BRONZE ALTAR — IInd-IIIrd Century A.D.   Acc.no. 37.1615E

PLATE 30. (ABOVE) IVORY INLAY — IVth-Vth Century A.D.
Acc.no. 37.1631E

(BELOW) BRONZE LAMP WITH CROSS — Vth-VIth Century A.D.
Acc.no. 16.133

PLATE 31. INCENSE BURNER, BRONZE — Vth Century A.D.
Acc.no. 41.684

PLATE 32. DETAIL OF RIM WITH DUCKS  Acc.no. 41.684

PLATE 33. LAMP WITH CROSS, ON STAND, BRONZE — VIth Century A.D.
Acc.no. 41.1086a-b

PLATE 34. CENSER WITH CRUCIFIXION OF CHRIST, BRONZE — VIth-VIIIth Century A.D.
Acc.no 42.94

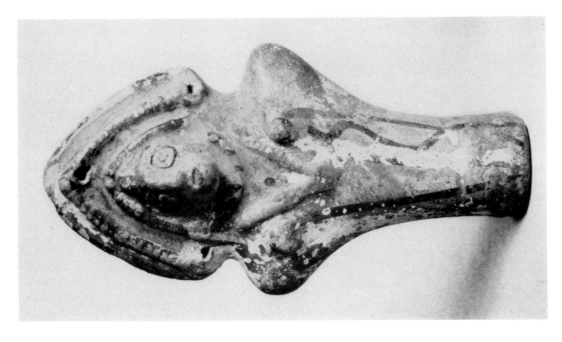

Acc.no. 16.161

Acc.no. 16.160

PLATE 35. TERRA COTTA STATUETTES – VIth-VIIth Century A.D.

PLATE 36. LARGE COPTIC POTTERY PLATE — VIth Century A.D.
Acc.no. 42.408

PLATE 37. STEATITE MOULD FOR AMULET WITH CRUCIFIXION — VIth-VIIth Century A.D.
Acc.no. 16.233

Acc.no. 37.1771E

PLATE 38. TEXTILES WITH GEOMETRIC DESIGNS – IIIrd-IVth Century A.D.

Acc.no. 26.735

Acc.no. 41.796

Acc.no. 41.794

Acc.no. 41.791

PLATE 39. COPTIC TEXTILES SHOWING LATE CLASSIC INFLUENCE
IVth-VIth Century A.D.

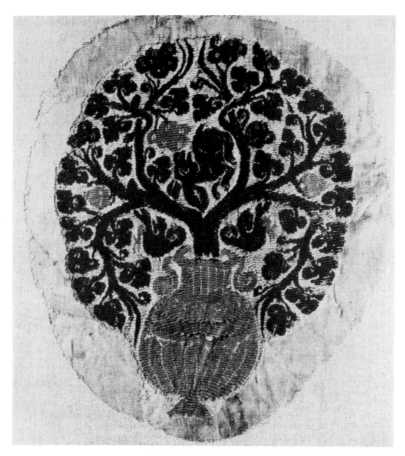

Acc.no. 42.438.1

Acc.no. 42.438.2

Acc.no. 42.438.4

PLATE 40. TEXTILES WITH CHARACTERISTIC COPTIC DESIGNS — IVth-VIth Century A.D.

Acc.no. 41.798

Acc.no. 41.810

Acc.no. 41.793

PLATE 41. COPTIC TEXTILES — IVth-VIIth Century A.D.

PLATE 42. BORDER WITH HALOED HEADS – IVth Century A.D. Acc.no. 38.684

PLATE 43. FRAGMENT OF A HANGING — IVth-Vth Century A.D.   Acc.no. 38.683

Acc.no. 08.480.52

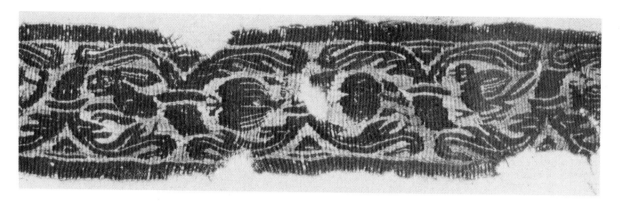

Acc.no. 41.797

Acc.no. 41.799

PLATE 44. BORDERS SHOWING ANIMALS IN FLORAL SCROLLS — IVth-VIIth Century A.D.

Acc.no. 41.812

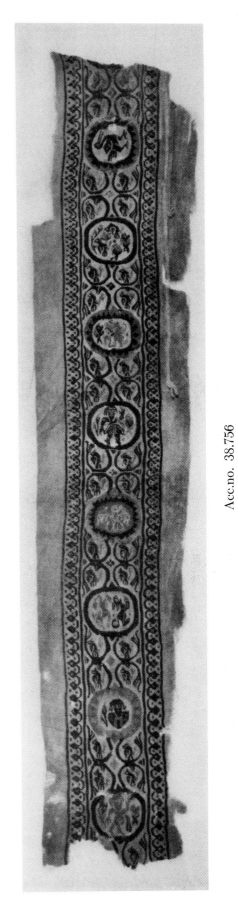

Acc.no. 38.756

PLATE 45. BANDS WITH HUMAN FIGURES, ANIMALS AND FLORAL MOTIFS — Vth-VIth Century A.D.

Acc.no. 15.440

Acc.no. 15.437

Acc.no. 15.443

Acc.no. 15.429

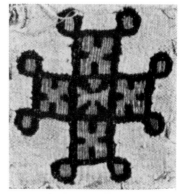

Acc.no. 15.439

PLATE 46. TEXTILES FROM ANTINOE — Vth-VIth Century A.D.

Plate 47. Fragments of Borders — IVth-VIth Century A.D.

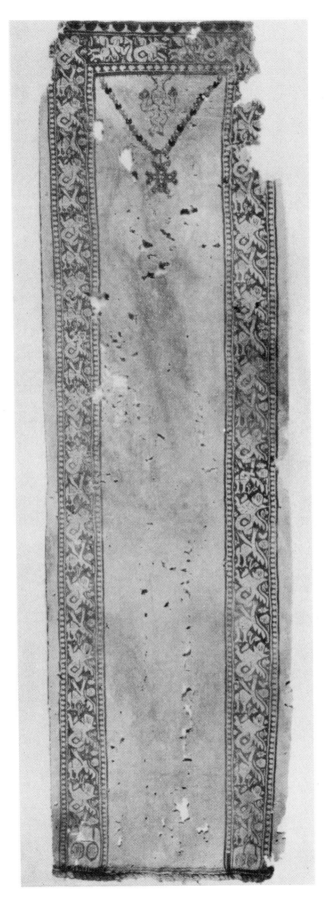

PLATE 48. TUNIC-FRONT — VIth Century A.D.
Acc.no. 38.753

PLATE 49. COPTIC TUNIC — VIIth Century A.D.   Acc.no. 41.523

PLATE 50. COPTIC TUNIC: DETAILS OF ORNAMENT    Acc.no. 41.523

PLATE 51. SQUARE WITH PORTRAIT BUST — VIth Century A.D.   Acc.no. 38.665

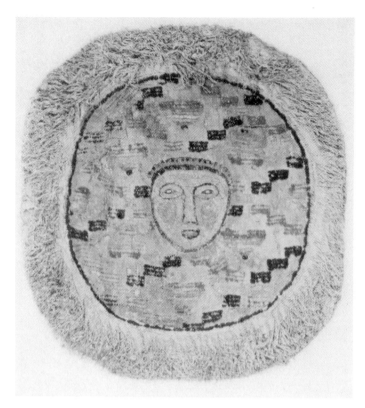

Acc.no. 26.753

Acc.no. 38.681    PLATE 52. COPTIC TEXTILES — IVth-VIth Century A.D.    Acc.no. 05.305

PLATE 53. TUNIC-FRONT WITH DECORATED BANDS — VIth Century A.D.
Acc.no. 38.748

Acc.no. 38.750                    Acc.no. 38.754

PLATE 54. TEXTILES WITH ARABIC INFLUENCE — VIIth-VIIIth Century A.D.